W9-AAM-426

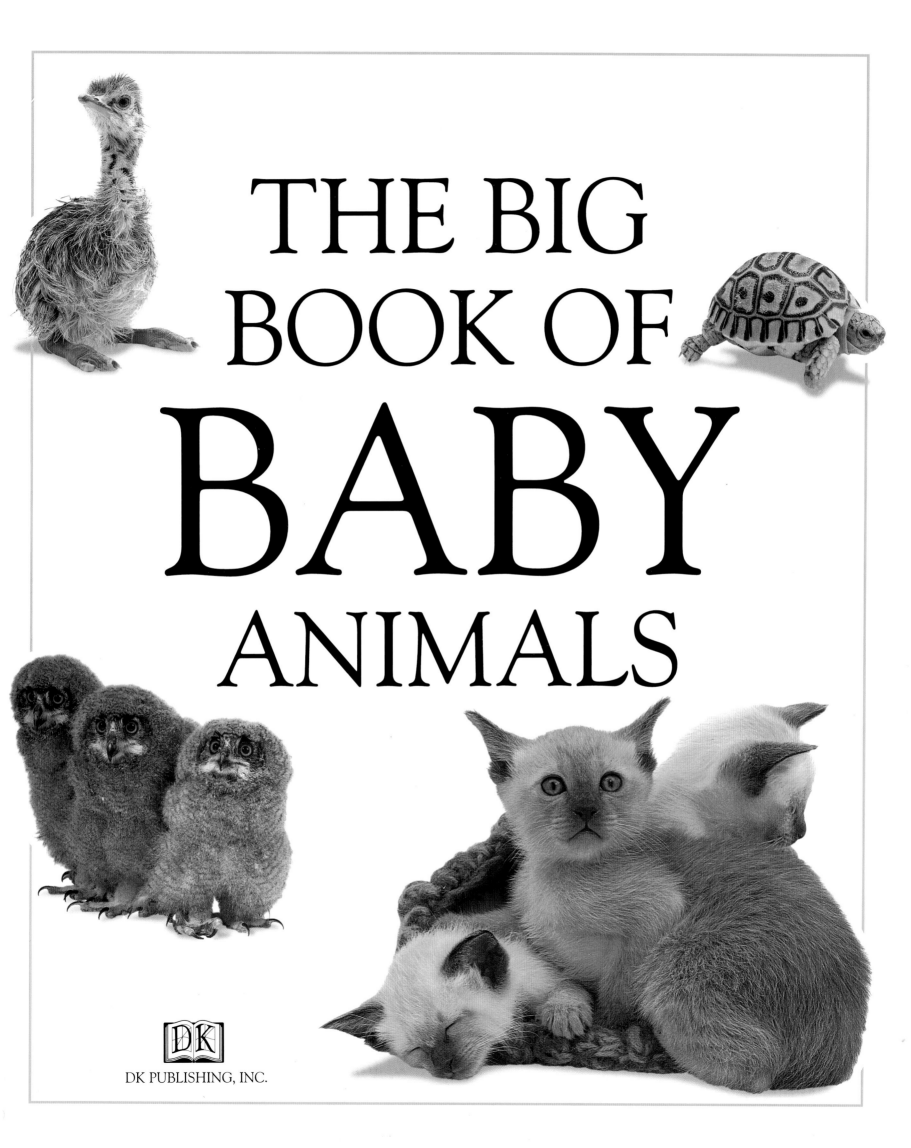

THE BIG
BOOK OF
BABY
ANIMALS

DK PUBLISHING, INC.

DK

A DK PUBLISHING BOOK

Writer and editor Nancy Jones
Art editor Diane Clouting
Illustrator Maggie Tingle
Senior managing editor Gillian Denton
Senior managing art editor Julia Harris
Picture researcher Catherine Edkins
Production Lisa Moss
DTP designer Nicky Studdart
US editors William Lach, Nicole Zarick

First American Edition, 1998
2 4 6 8 10 9 7 5 3

Published in the United States by
DK Publishing, Inc. 95 Madison Avenue New York, New York 10016
Visit us on the World Wide Web at http://www.dk.com

Copyright © 1998 Dorling Kindersley Limited, London

All rights reserved under International and Pan-American Copyright Conventions. No part of this
publication may be reproduced, stored in a retrieval system, or transmitted in any form or by any means,
electronic, mechanical, photocopying, recording, or otherwise, without the prior written permission of
the copyright owner. Published in Great Britain by Dorling Kindersley Limited.

Library of Congress Cataloging-in-Publication Data

The big book of baby animals.
p. cm.
Summary: Text and illustrations present information about the physical
characteristics, behavior, and development of baby animals, from tiny mice
and dozy hamsters to frolicking fawns and purring pumas.
ISBN 0-7894-3069-x

1. Animals – Infancy – Juvenile literature. [1. Animals – Infancy]
I. DK Publishing, Inc.
QL763.B8 1998
591.3'9–dc21

Color reproduction by Pica Overseas Ltd.
Printed and bound in Spain by Artes Gráficas Toledo, S.A.
D.L. TO: 1199 - 1999

Contents

Family likeness

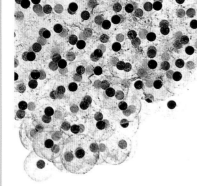

Like mother like baby

Some babies look like their parents when they are born, but others, like frogs, have to wait until they become adults. Just like you, every animal in this book is unique, similar but not quite the same as its mother or its father.

The female frog finds a pond and lays her eggs.

The babies live in the pond and are called tadpoles. These tadpoles have already grown tiny legs. Slowly they are turning into frogs.

After three months, the tadpole has become a frog. It has left the pond and lives on land.

To its mother, every piglet is different from its brothers and sisters.

A little bit different

These piglets have just been born. They look a lot like their mother, but not exactly the same. The mother pig has black patches on her pink skin, but her babies are pink all over.

The baby mona monkey has a blue face, just like its mother.

Big family

Mona monkeys live together in big groups. Each group is made up of many females and one male, who is the father of most of the babies in the group.

Big change

When a butterfly baby hatches from its egg as a caterpillar, it's hard to believe it will ever look like its splendid parents.

The caterpillar will soon hatch out of its egg.

The caterpillar eats and eats, getting bigger every day.

The caterpillar grows a hard case called a chrysalis. Two weeks later it emerges as a beautiful butterfly.

Independent baby

When a baby giraffe is a few months old, it often wanders away from its mother and spends its time with other giraffes. It always comes back eventually though, to drink its mother's warm milk.

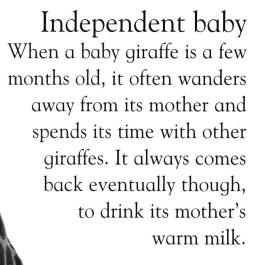

When the baby is older, its coat will be as dark as its mother's.

All kinds of babies

Amazing change

Like many insects, when a ladybug baby hatches from its egg, it doesn't look like its parents at all. It eats as much as it can, getting ready for its magical change into an adult ladybug.

The eggs are laid underneath a leaf. After a week the baby ladybugs hatch out.

Baby ladybugs are called larvae.

The baby grows a hard case. Inside the case, its body dissolves and then re-forms in the shape of an adult ladybug.

Healthy milk

These kittens have just been born. Now they are drinking their mother's milk. She takes good care of them, keeping them warm and safe, and feeding them when they are hungry.

All babies that drink milk are called mammals.

In the sea

Dogfish lay their eggs inside tough cases that they attach to seaweed by the long, curly string in each corner. When the baby fish wriggles out of the egg, it is ready to take care of itself.

Dogfish live in the sea.

Baby birds are called chicks.

Little chick

This chick grew inside an egg that its parents sat on to keep warm. Now it is two days old. It doesn't drink milk like a kitten, instead its parents teach it to catch tasty insects.

Some snakes' eggs have soft shells.

Slithery baby

Snakes don't need to look after their babies. Many snakes lay eggs and when the young snakes hatch out they slither away.

This young newt is four weeks old.

Out of the water

Baby newts live in water, but adult newts live mainly on land. This young newt still lives in water, but it already has tiny legs for walking. Soon it will grow lungs too and will climb out of the water to live on land.

Somewhere to live

These babies will soon leave the nest.

Crowded house

The parents of these young blue titmice used twigs, dry grass, and feathers to build a cozy nest, hidden away in the branches of a tree.

Foxy faces

A fox uses its sharp claws and strong legs to dig its den. These cubs are waiting for their parents to come home with something to eat.

A fox's den is called an earth.

Plenty of room

This mole is ready to give birth to her babies. She has lined her underground nest with grass and leaves to keep the babies warm and dry.

Moles live alone. The second mole is an intruder, hoping to steal earthworms from the food storage.

Living nursery

A kangaroo doesn't build a nest or a burrow. Instead, the baby lives in its mother's pouch, where it drinks milk from her nipple. By the time it is ten months old, the baby will be too big to fit inside the pouch.

A baby kangaroo is called a joey.

A squirrel's nest is the size of a soccer ball.

Well built

Wedged firmly in the fork of a branch, this nest will make a cozy home for the squirrel through the cold winter. In early spring, three or four babies will be born in the nest.

9

Motherly care

Bamboo breakfast

A panda cub lives with its mother until it is a year and a half old. This young panda has already left its mother. It eats bamboo all day long.

This young cuckoo has grown too big to fit into the nest.

Oversize baby

A cuckoo lays its eggs in another bird's nest. The young cuckoo's new parents feed it with insects. Even when the baby is bigger than the parents, they still think it is their own chick.

Easy does it

This cat is carrying her kitten in her mouth without biting it. Each kitten has its own smell, which helps its mother to recognize it.

The kitten cannot see or hear yet.

Heavy load

As soon as they are born, the baby scorpions climb onto their mother's back. For two weeks they cling tightly with their tiny claws. Then they jump off and walk by themselves.

The scorpions are three days old.

The baby holds tightly to its mother's fur.

Nice view

The safest place for a baby gorilla is on its mother's back. Together they walk through the jungle looking for tasty plants to eat.

Well cared for

The mother hen sits on her eggs for 21 days while the chicks grow inside. These chicks are two weeks old. If danger threatens, the hen will flap her wings and look fierce, while the chicks run away and hide safely.

The chicks follow their mother wherever she goes.

How many babies?

Family fortunes

All animals have babies. Some have lots of babies and don't take care of them at all. Others have just a few babies and look after them carefully to make sure that they survive.

A zebra gives birth to a single foal, which it looks after very carefully.

These babies will leave their mother when they are only a few weeks old.

Quick turnover

Many mice get eaten by their enemies. The solution is to have lots of babies. A female mouse can give birth to one hundred babies in a year.

Dangerous times

Some turtles lay as many as a hundred eggs. The female turtle buries the eggs then leaves them. When they hatch, the babies look after themselves.

From a hundred eggs, only a few turtles will survive to adulthood.

A koala can only carry one baby.

Only one

A koala carries her baby around with her for almost a year. When it is very tiny it lives in her pouch. Later it rides on her back, hanging on tightly as she climbs through the trees.

A lot to learn

An orangutan baby lives with its mother until it is eight years old. She teaches it to recognize more than 200 different plants.

An orangutan has only one baby every seven years.

Big family

When a female rabbit gives birth, she produces seven or eight babies. Newborn rabbits are tiny but they grow very quickly. By the time they are four months old, the young are able to have babies themselves.

These babies are four weeks old.

13

On the farm

All baby birds grow inside eggs.

Cheep! Cheep!

These chicks are three days old. They can already feed themselves by pecking up seeds and insects. If they get cold, they hide among their mother's warm feathers.

Water babies

Ducklings love to swim in the pond with their mother. They dip their beaks in the water, looking for tasty plants and insects to eat.

Golden gosling

It takes about 30 days for a gosling to hatch from its egg. The mother sits on the eggs, while the father stands guard.

Newborn gosling.

The calves are two months old.

Dinner time

In addition to eating straw and hay, these two young calves drink their mother's creamy milk. The rich milk helps them to grow fast.

Lambs are born in the spring.

Natural acrobats

Wild goats live high up in the mountains. These baby goats live on a farm, but they will soon be able to climb and jump as well as wild goats.

Baby goats are called kids.

Up and about

These lambs have just been born, but they are already strong enough to stand up. They love to drink their mother's milk.

Cabbage is a good food for hungry pigs.

Sleepy piglets

These little piglets are two days old. Their mother will soon come to feed them. Then they will all fall asleep, snuggling up together to keep warm.

Forest and woodland

Growing up fast

When mice are born, they are blind and deaf and have no fur. They keep warm by snuggling together in their cozy nest. Now this tiny mouse is two weeks old. Its fur has grown and it can see and hear well.

In a few weeks this mouse might have babies of its own.

Foxes eat all kinds of eggs.

Hungry fox

Newborn cubs stay in the den, drinking their mother's milk. This little fox is six weeks old, ready to explore the outside world.

Shy fawn

A fawn's long legs help it to run fast to escape from enemies. Its spotted coat makes it hard to see as it hides among the trees.

Baby deer are called fawns or kids.

Young badgers like to play.

Home underground

Badgers live far underground in deep burrows. The babies are born blind and helpless and don't come to the surface until they are two months old.

Good hunter

A tawny owl lays its eggs in a hole in a tree. When the chicks hatch, their parents catch mice for them to eat. Soon they will teach the chicks to fly.

This chick can swallow a mouse whole.

A chipmunk holds food in its paws.

Leaving home

This chipmunk is six weeks old and has just left the underground den where it was born. It likes to eat nuts, worms, and mushrooms.

Cuddly cubs

Baby bears are born in their mother's winter den as she dozes through the freezing weather. They drink her milk until spring comes. Then the whole family goes out into the forest to look for food.

The cubs stay with their mother for a year and a half.

Sharp senses

Kittens are born blind and deaf, but with a good sense of smell. At two weeks old their eyes and ears open, and they can see and hear very well.

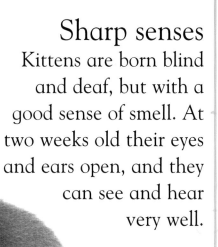

A kitten can see in the dark.

Natural hunter

This nine-week-old kitten is creeping up silently on one of its sisters. With plenty of practice, it will soon be ready to try hunting for mice and birds.

Well-washed kitten

Cats and kittens spend lots of time licking and wiping their fur to keep it in good condition. The mother cat teaches her kittens how to keep themselves clean.

Kittens love to wash themselves.

Leopard cats
live in jungles.

Wide awake

This kitten stays awake much longer now than it did when it was younger. Even when it is an adult cat, though, it will spend more than half of its time fast asleep.

The kitten
is eight
weeks old.

Unusual mixture

Part domestic cat, and part wild-leopard cat, this kitten has inherited the leopard spots of its wild ancestors.

Eye on the ball

Chasing a small ball is a popular game for kittens, because the ball seems to run away, just like a mouse. This brother and sister are ready to play with their favorite toy.

Playing helps kittens
learn the skills they will
need in adult life.

Wild cats

Purring puma

By the time it is a year old, this baby puma will have lost its spots and turned a pale gold. A puma cannot roar like a lion, but it can purr and meow, just like a pet cat.

When it gets hot, a puma likes to cool off by lying in the river.

White tiger

Most tigers are golden with black stripes. Occasionally a baby is born which is white instead, like this one. A tiger cub never sees its father. It lives with its mother until it is about 18 months old. Then it leaves home to live on its own.

Climbing leopard

Leopards live in all sorts of places, including mountains, forests, and jungles. Leopards are very good at climbing trees. They often drag their food up into the branches where they can eat it in peace.

This leopard cub is four months old.

Tiger cubs are blind until they are two weeks old.

Stripy coat

This cub is ten weeks old. It still drinks its mother's milk, but soon she will start to teach it how to hunt. Tigers are so strong that they can kill almost anything, except an elephant.

Tigers are good swimmers.

This lion cub is three weeks old.

Lovely lion

Lions live together in groups called prides, helping each other hunt for food. All the females help look after the cubs. Baby lions are born with spots on their coats which disappear as they grow older.

Playful puppies

Golden baby

Labradors come in three colors, yellow like this little puppy, chocolate-brown, and black. Labradors love to swim. They have thick, waterproof fur, which keeps them dry and warm in the coldest water.

Labradors make good guide dogs for the blind.

Police dog

When this puppy is older it will work with the police, helping them to catch criminals.

German shepherds are very strong and intelligent.

This brother and sister are eight weeks old.

Playtime

Puppies love to play. Not only do they have fun, they learn how to get along together. If they get too rough, their mother will give them a sharp nip.

Little lion

This puppy comes from China. Because its long hair looks like a lion's mane, it's name is shih tzu, which means "little lion." Even when it is fully grown, a shih tzu is still small enough to carry in one hand.

The puppy's ears are very long.

This puppy's long hair is often tied up in a pony tail.

Energetic pup

This spaniel puppy is exercising its sharp teeth on its new toy. Spaniels are strong and active. They love to play all kinds of energetic games.

New arrivals

All puppies are blind and deaf when they are born. Until they are a week old all they can do is to drink their mother's milk and snuggle up against her to sleep.

This dachshund puppy's short legs make it good at squeezing into all kinds of holes.

Perfect pets

Underground living

Wild hamsters live in hot, rocky deserts. During the day they stay cool in underground burrows. The burrow has long tunnels and lots of different rooms, including a nest for the babies and storage for food.

Young hamsters like to play together.

A donkey's long ears help it stay cool in hot weather.

Little donkey

Donkeys resemble horses, but they are much smaller. Donkeys are descendants of wild asses, which live in Africa.

White and fluffy

This little rabbit is five weeks old. Soon it will be ready to leave its mother and its brothers and sisters. Wild rabbits live in burrows deep underground.

Long-legged foal

It takes a whole year for a foal to grow inside its mother. This foal is five weeks old. Its legs are very long to help it run fast.

Three little pigs

Newborn guinea pigs look just like tiny adults. They can see and hear, and have a thick, warm coat. They can crawl around immediately. After a few days, they start to eat grass and other solid foods. Wild guinea pigs live in South America.

Baby guinea pigs are called puppies.

On safari

Drink up

This rhino calf is four weeks old. It will stay with its mother until her next baby is born in two years. It drinks lots of her milk to help it grow fast.

When the baby is older it will grow two strong horns.

Long legs

Ostriches are the biggest birds in the world. They cannot fly, but they can run very fast. This chick could grow to be eight feet tall – taller than a basketball player.

This chick is three days old.

Playful elephant

Baby elephants can walk almost as soon as they are born. They follow the other elephants as they search for plants to eat. When they are not drinking their mother's milk, baby elephants love to play together.

It takes nearly two years for a baby elephant to grow inside its mother.

This baby is ready for its first taste of leaves.

Stretching tall

A giraffe's tongue is longer than your arm. Its legs and neck are long too, so it can reach high into trees to eat tasty leaves and fruit. When it is born, a baby giraffe is already as tall as an adult.

Every giraffe has a different pattern on its coat.

Special stripes

Young zebras have brown stripes that turn black as they grow up. A baby zebra keeps close to its mother. It recognizes her by the pattern of her stripes.

Zebras live on grassy plains.

Life in cold places

Where on earth?

At the very top and the very bottom of the earth, there are two huge, cold areas, called the Arctic, in the north, and the Antarctic, in the south. All the animals that live in these places have special ways of keeping warm.

This reindeer calf has thick, waterproof fur and sharp hooves to stop it from slipping on the ice.

Summer colors

This young arctic fox has a brown coat. When winter comes it will grow a thick white coat, which keeps it warm and makes it difficult to see in the snow.

Arctic foxes eat small rodents called lemmings.

Polar bears have very thick fur to keep them warm.

Hungry hunters

Baby polar bears are born underground in a cozy den dug in the snow. The cubs and their mother stay in the den until winter is over. In spring the whole family hunts for seals on the frozen Arctic sea.

This snowy owl's black and white feathers help her stay hidden while she sits on the nest.

Keeping snug

A female snowy owl makes her nest by digging a small hollow with her feet. When the chicks hatch out, their mother keeps them warm, while their father hunts for food.

The chicks' favorite food is raw squid.

Antarctic king

King penguin chicks live in huge groups, snuggling together to keep warm through the icy weather. These chicks are two months old. Their parents leave them on the shore while they swim far out to sea to catch fish and squid. It will be nearly a year before the chicks learn to fish for themselves.

A watery home

Fluffy moorhens

These chicks are black and fluffy now, but as adults they will look very different. Their bodies will be brown and gray, and their legs will be bright green.

The chicks are only one day old.

Fishing practice

This family of otters lives in a hole in the river bank. The cubs can already swim well, but it will be another year before they can catch as many fish as their mother does.

Friendly hippopotamus

Hippos live together in large groups. This female is surrounded by babies, but only one is hers. The hippos keep cool in the river during the day and feed on grass at night.

Hippos live in Africa.

Sea lions are closely related to seals.

Plump pup

Adult sea lions spend most of their time swimming in the sea, where they hunt for fish and octopus. When they get tired they come ashore to rest. This sea lion pup is growing fast, drinking lots of its mother's rich milk.

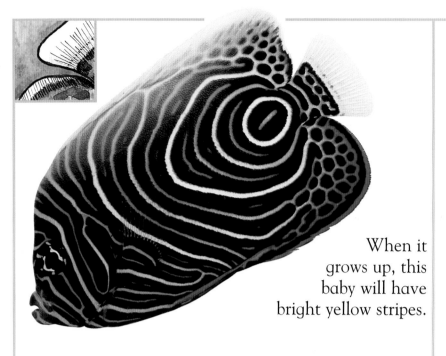

When it grows up, this baby will have bright yellow stripes.

Little emperor

This young emperor angel fish lives in the warm sea around a coral reef. A reef is a living wall, made of millions of tiny animals called corals. The angel fish eats the coral and hides in it, too.

Patient hunter

Even though it has just hatched from its egg, this baby caiman can already look after itself. It lies hidden in the water, waiting to catch juicy insects with a quick snap of its jaws.

A newly-hatched caiman is as long as your finger.

Good mother

When a baby dolphin is born, its mother looks after it very carefully. She teaches it how to swim and how to breathe through its blowhole. The baby stays close by its mother's side until it is more than a year old.

Big-headed baby

This baby big-headed turtle is very unusual because its head is so big that it cannot tuck it inside its shell when it wants to hide from its enemies.

This turtle lives in a mountain stream.

Index

Acknowledgments

Photography for DK by: Neil Fletcher, Kim Taylor, Geoff Brightling, Peter Anderson, Bill Ling, Jane Burton, Jerry Young, Mike Linley, Jon Bouchier, Gordon Clayton, Steve Shott, Tracy Morgan, Barrie Watts, Paul Bricknell, Steve Gorton, Marc Henrie, Gary Huggins, Dave King, Frank Greenaway, Peter Downs, Robin Forbes, Mike Dunning, Karl Shone.

The publisher would like to thank the following for kind permission to reproduce their photographs:
c=center; t=top; b=bottom; l=left; r=right
Heather Angel: 10tl; Bruce Coleman: Jeff Foott Productions 8tr; Mr. Johnny Johnson 28b; Frank Lane Picture Agency: L. Chace 12bl; Natural History Photographic Agency: Hellio and Van Ingen 29tl; B. Jones and M. Shimlock 31cbelow; Gerard Lacz 24bl; Oxford Scientific Films: Norbert Rosing 28tr; Planet Earth Pictures: Gary Bell 9tl; C. Denis-Huot 30bl; Geoff du Feu 30tr; Telegraph Colour Library: 13tl; Barrie Watts: 12tr, 12/13bc, 14tr, 16tl, 25tl; Jerry Young: 7bl, 20t.